CHILD BRAIN DEVELOPMENT
An Active Learning Approach

Summer Howell

Table of Content

CHAPTER 1

How to raise a smart and a happy child

What is typically the most common response when you ask parents what they want for their children? They desire the happiness of their kids.

Adults place a higher priority on children's safety than almost anything else, including senior citizens' health, the cost of living, terrorism, and the Iraq War. Concerning children's welfare, more than two-thirds of adults say they are "extremely concerned," and this concern is shared by people of all ages, genders, socioeconomic backgrounds, and political views.

It can be challenging to strike a balance between what's best for kids and what makes them happy, but the two don't always have to go hand in hand.

Happier children have a higher chance of becoming successful, accomplished adults.

In a society where performance is valued highly, happiness is a huge advantage.

What parenting practices result in content children?

1 Make yourself happy

Ironically, being a little selfish is the first step to happier kids.

Your level of happiness has a significant impact on how content and successful your children are.

Numerous studies have found a strong connection between depressed mothers and "negative outcomes" in their kids, like acting out and other behavioral issues. Behavioral issues in children seem to be a direct result of parental depression, which also reduces the effectiveness of our parenting.

And it's not just genetics that's to blame. The study did discover that happy parents are statistically more likely to have happy children, but it was unable to identify any genetic basis for this relationship.

What then should you do to start living a happier life? Spend some time with friends having fun each week.

Hang out with friends or family who are likely to be laughing themselves because laughter is contagious. Their laughter will make you laugh as well, though it isn't even necessary for your mood to become lighter. According to neuroscientists, listening to someone else laugh activates mirror neurons in a part of the brain that gives listeners the impression that they are laughing as well.

Here are more evidence-based ways to make you happier.

2. **Instruct them in developing relationships**

No one disputes the significance of learning about relationships, but how many parents take the time to teach their children how to relate to others?

(Simply telling children to "knock it off" when they fight won't help them develop important social skills.)

It doesn't require much. Encourage children to carry out small deeds of kindness to foster empathy as a starting point.

In the long run, according to research, this not only helps your children become better people and develop necessary skills, but it also makes them happier.

Over two years, MS patients who underwent training to offer monthly 15-minute phone calls to other MS patients to whom they could show compassion and unconditional positive regard "showed pronounced improvement in self-confidence, self-esteem, depression, and role functioning." These caregivers received extra protection from anxiety and depression.

More on developing strong connections here.

3. Aim for effort instead of perfection

Tiger Moms and helicopter perfectionist parents, take note: chill out.

Kids get into trouble when parents constantly beat the achievement drum.

Compared to other parents, those who place an excessive emphasis on achievement are more likely to have children who experience high levels of anxiety, depression, and substance abuse.

Praise effort, not natural ability, according to the research, which is very consistent.

Most of the children who had been praised for their intelligence preferred the simpler puzzle because they didn't want to risk making a mistake and losing their reputation as intelligent children. On the other hand, more than 90% of children who were encouraged to adopt a growth mindset chose a more difficult puzzle.

Why? According to Dweck, when we commend children for their effort and hard work, which results in success, they are motivated to continue using those methods. They are not distracted from their task of learning by worries about how smart they may or may not appear to be.

Here's more information on how to praise effectively.

4. Instill optimism

Want to stay away from a grumpy teen? Then instruct those preteens to see the positive side of things.

When they later go through puberty, ten-year-olds who are taught to think and interpret the world optimistically are half as likely to experience depression.

Simply put, according to author Christine Carter, "optimism and happiness are practically equivalent."

When she contrasts optimists and pessimists, she discovers that:

are more productive at work, school, and sports

are happier in their marriages, live longer, and are healthier

less prone to experience depression and anxiety

Here's more advice on how to promote optimism.

5. Educate on emotional intelligence

A skill rather than an innate quality, emotional intelligence.

It doesn't set kids up for success to believe they will "naturally" learn to understand their own emotions, let alone those of others.

When someone is struggling with anger or frustration, a straightforward first step is to "Empathize, Label, and Validate."

"I am SO SO SO MAD AT YOU," said Molly.

You're furious with me, I can tell that much. Please elaborate. Are you also disappointed that I'm not allowing you to go on a playdate right now?

Yes, Molly. I'm ready for a playdate right now.

"You seem sad," I said. Molly (whimpers a little and rests her head on my shoulder while crawling into my lap.)

Relate to the child, assist them in recognizing their feelings, and reassure them that they are acceptable (even though bad behavior might not be).

Find out more about labeling and active listening (and how hostage negotiators employ these techniques) here.

6. Develop Happy Habits

We've reached step 6, and you might feel that there is already a lot to remember, let alone for a young person. With the right habits, we can get past that.

Although considering these strategies requires effort, once habits are formed, acting habitually is simple.

How can you assist kids in forming enduring happiness habits? Carter outlines a few potent techniques supported by evidence:

Eliminate distractions and temptations to remove stimuli.
Make It Known: Set objectives to increase social pressure and support.
One Objective at a Time Willpower is weakened by having too many goals, especially in children. First, establish one habit, then add another.

Keep going: Don't expect success right away. It requires time. Relapses will happen. That is typical. Continue reiterating.
More on forming virtuous habits here.

7. Instill Self-Control

In children, self-control is a better indicator of success than intelligence or almost any other factor.
Yes, it's time for the infamous marshmallow test once more. Children who were better able to resist temptation went on to live much better lives and were happier as adults

The ability of preschoolers to postpone gratification—to wait for that second marshmallow—predicts adolescent intelligence, academic success, and social skills. This is due, at least in part, to the fact that self-control makes it easier to learn and process information. Additionally, disciplined children are more likely to feel a greater sense of social responsibility and can handle stress and frustration better. In other words, self-control promotes greater happiness, more friends, and greater involvement in the community in addition to academic success and manners at the dinner table.

What would be an effective way to start teaching self-control? Aid children in learning to deter temptation.

One strategy is to physically hide the tempting marshmallow to hide the temptation. In one study, 75% of children could wait a full fifteen minutes for the second marshmallow when the reward was hidden; none of the children could wait this long when the reward was visible.

Here's more information on boosting self-control.

8. **Additional Playtime**

These days, we read a lot about mindfulness and meditation, and both are very effective.

But it can be difficult to get kids to do them frequently. What functions nearly as well?

More time to play.

When they play, most children already engage in mindfulness, which is fully appreciating the present moment. however, modern children play less both inside and outside. In total, children have lost eight hours of free, spontaneous play every week over the past 20 years.

Play is more than just having fun. Children need it to develop and learn.

Researchers think that this sharp decline in free play time is partly to blame for children's slower emotional and cognitive growth. Child-led, unstructured play (with or without adults) promoted mental, physical, social, and emotional health in addition to helping kids learn to self-regulate. Unstructured play teaches kids how to cooperate with others, share, compromise, settle disputes, control their emotions and behavior, and speak up for themselves.

No specific guidelines are required in this case: Increase the amount of time you allot for your kids to play outdoors.

Read more about the benefits of playing for both children and adults here.

9. Modify Their Environment to Make Them Happy

We don't like to admit it, but our environments have a significant impact on all of us—often more than we realize.

Time and effort constraints will limit your efforts, whereas we (and children) are constantly impacted by context.
What easy steps can you take to better manage a child's environment so that your deliberate happiness efforts have the greatest impact?
lower TV.

Research shows a direct correlation between happiness and avoiding television. Researchers in sociology have found that happier people typically watch a lot less television than unhappy people. Whether watching TV makes people unhappy or if unhappy people watch more TV is unknown. However, we are aware that numerous activities can support our children's growth into content, well-adjusted adults. If our children are watching TV, they aren't engaging in activities that might ultimately make them happier.

Here are some more enjoyable activities outside of television.

10. **Share a meal**

Sometimes science does nothing more than confirm what our ancestors already knew. Family dinner does matter.
This straightforward custom makes kids happier and helps them develop into better people.

According to studies, children who regularly eat dinner with their families are more emotionally stable and are less likely to abuse drugs and alcohol. They received higher grades. Particularly among adolescent girls, they exhibit fewer depressive symptoms. Additionally, they are less likely to develop an eating disorder or to become obese. Even reading to your children is surpassed by family dinners in terms of preparing them for school. And these relationships persist even after researchers take family ties into account.

CHAPTER 2

How the brain and mind develop in the first five

5 Year-Olds: Development & Growth
Children under 5 years old

Introduction
Your young child is developing an identity, making new friends, and visiting new locations! The activities and developmental milestones that are enabling your child to get along with others, partake in more complex play, and take a greater role in taking care of themselves are detailed in this chapter.

Learn about the brain of your young child. Their cells are connected in intricate ways.

small children

For both you and your child, this is a year of change. Starting kindergarten is a big step, even for kids who are accustomed to daycare or preschool. Your child is growing more able to pay attention for longer periods and is more eager to learn. They now inquire not only "Why," but also "What if."

Every child develops at their own pace, and they might have a different growth pattern from their siblings and friends. Furthermore, you can anticipate that they'll:

grow in spurts—they might appear to be the same size for weeks before suddenly growing taller almost immediately. They also get stronger and more eager to try out their new skills as their body develops.

Developmental Benchmarks

Your young child is making more new friends and visiting new locations. They will gain more social skills as they enter kindergarten and develop new relationships. They'll start to feel more at ease and confident being by themselves, around other kids, and in strange environments. Your child will still require your warm support as they venture farther from home and when they return to you with their fresh ideas and inquiries.

Your young child will be eager to learn, try new things, and start to develop a longer attention span as they turn 5 years old. Your child can move more purposefully and deftly. You can read more about the tasks and developmental milestones your child is working on below, between the ages of 5 and 6.

The "identity" and "power" stage for 5-year-olds Tasks

Your child is learning the following at this time in addition to continuing to practice earlier tasks:

- Form an identity by beginning to understand oneself and one's place in the world
- Acknowledge personal power learn that they are in charge of what they do and that what they do affects other people
- Build industry learn to enjoy the inquiry-based nature of problem-solving

MILESTONES: PHYSICAL

- Has stronger muscles, increases coordination, and complex skills
- Moves more purposefully and accurately

- Enjoys being active,
- Draws, and begins printing letters,
- but may require more sleep due to school demands

MILESTONES: SOCIAL

- Increases their desire to win,
- Enjoys playing games with rules,
- Has a best friend,
- Has more adults in their life who can influence them, such as teachers and coaches.

MILESTONES: EMOTIONAL

- A better understanding of right and wrong
- Begins to speak aloud to themselves to calm down;

- Dislikes correction;
- Gets easily upset by things that are unfair or 'not right

MILESTONES: COGNITIVE (THINKING AND COMMUNICATING) (THINKING AND COMMUNICATING)

- Has more time to focus
- Talks in greater detail
- Use complete sentences and proper grammar
- Uses the majority of the words in sentences that you, your siblings, friends, and strangers can understand, and enjoys telling jokes and riddles.
- Starts to comprehend death and may have many inquiries about it.

DEVELOPING THE BRAIN

Your young child will experience a lot of changes quickly, pick up a lot of new skills, and enjoy being active. They are developing new ways of thinking, going through difficult emotions, and learning how to get along with others. Your young child's development in all areas is interconnected, and changes in one area have an impact on changes in all other areas. The brain of your child directs their growth.

Knowing how the brain functions make it simpler to comprehend what you can do to support your child.

A picture of a brain is surrounded by the names of four interconnected developmental domains: physical, emotional, social, and cognitive.

Your young child's brain is currently undergoing rapid development, and the connections between brain cells are becoming more intricate. Strong foundations have been built through enduring relationships with you and other significant individuals in their lives.

Executive function abilities, which are crucial for learning and interacting with others, are now being developed in the brain. Your child is beginning to demonstrate the following abilities, though it will take some time for them to fully develop:

- Observe how their body is responding to stress,
- Sometimes being able to manage those feelings on their own, and remember information to use when necessary

- The capacity to concentrate on a task without getting distracted and manage their impulses
- Thinking and feeling as circumstances change

One of the most crucial lessons you can impart to your child is how to self-regulate when they are under stress. It serves as the cornerstone for healthy living, lifelong learning, and executive function. Find out more about self-control.

You can teach your child to develop executive function skills in a variety of entertaining ways, including by having them wait, use their memory, and learn about emotions.

CHAPTER 3

How does education helps in the development of a child

Today's youth are preparing to become tomorrow's adults and citizens. The quality of the current educational system reflects growth, which is parallel to the future of our nation. Young, impressionable minds need to be piqued with curiosity, and schools need to give them the tools they need to become better people.

It is generally acknowledged that education plays a significant role in determining a person's personality and approach to life's challenges. In schools, there has been a sea change due to the shift in emphasis from bookish knowledge to life knowledge. People are becoming more open to the idea that education is essential for well-rounded development rather than just a way to earn degrees and succeed financially in life. Our cognitive abilities must be developed and a healthy thought process must be encouraged through education. Education, along with food, clothing, and shelter, is a basic human need in the modern, competitive world.

The following areas must be emphasized in school instruction because they have a significant impact on how young minds develop as they approach adulthood.

1. MENTAL COMPONENT

The primary source of knowledge that children encounter in school. It offers them the chance to learn about many different areas of education, including people, literature, history, math, politics, and many other topics. The cultivation of the mind is aided by this. When someone is exposed to influences from different cultural sources, their perspective of the world and their existence expand.

2 SOCIAL COMPONENT

A child's first opportunity to make friends is at school. The child has only interacted with his or her parents and close relatives up until that point. Additionally, familiarity breeds complacency. Children are exposed to new ideas in schools, as well as their peers their age. This instills social skills like empathy, friendship, participation, and assistance which are crucial for them as adults.

3. PHYSICAL QUALITY

A child develops physically in a variety of ways after conception. While a child's home environment only offers a limited outlet, the school allows him to focus his energy on more sociable pursuits. According to studies, children learn to behave best when around other kids their age, even though they are capable of handling sudden bursts of energy in a familiar environment. Additionally, familiarity encourages exploiting circumstances, whereas in school the playing field is level. Additionally, the availability of activities like sports and crafts encourages kids to channel their boundless energy toward something positive.

overall progress

In the past, schools were thought of as places where students learned about historical events, tackled challenging mathematical problems, or memorized sonnets. A child learns to go beyond the traditional method of rote learning in the current educational environment. They are taught to form their own opinions, and the flexible curriculum encourages inquiry. The child is set free from the restrictions of mental blocks and is allowed to let his or her imagination run wild. The value of imagination is emphasized frequently. A cognitive system that is well-developed is the result of play activities and a comprehensive curriculum.

In addition to living, life is also about learning. Our parents can teach us a lot, but they often make decisions all by themselves. Children are exposed to a variety of sources at school from which they can learn a vast amount of information that is essential to their development. Therefore, school is essential for teaching kids about how the world works

CHAPTER 4

Strategies to nuture your child development

Some children appear to have higher self-esteem than others, but there are many things you can do to support your child's emotional health. A higher sense of self can help your child be more emotionally resilient when difficulties arise.

The physical needs of your child (food, shelter, clothing) can be met quite easily. It can be more difficult to try to meet your child's emotional needs. Despite the wide variety of parenting approaches, the majority of experts concur on a few general principles for promoting a child's emotional well-being and laying the foundation for an emotionally healthy adulthood.

- Understand the stages of a child's development so you don't place excessive or unreasonable demands on them.

- Encourage your child to express his or her emotions while also showing respect for them. Tell your child that everyone feels hurt, afraid, angry, and anxious. Find out where these feelings are coming from. Encourage your child to express anger in healthy ways rather than using force.

- Promote trust and respect between people. Even when you disagree, keep your voice at a reasonable volume. Keep the lines of communication open.

- Pay attention to your kid. Use language and examples that your child can comprehend. Encourage inquiry. Convey consolation and assurance. Be truthful. Consider the advantages. Declare that you are open to discussing any topic.

- Examine your own coping and problem-solving techniques. Do you set a good example for others? If your child's emotions or behaviors are overwhelming you or if you find it difficult to control your annoyance or rage, seek help.

- Support your child's abilities while accepting their limitations. Instead of basing your goals on what you think will happen, consider the child's interests and abilities. Commemorate successes. Respect your child's individuality rather than compare their skills to those of other kids. Regularly spend time with your child.
- Encourage your child's autonomy and self-worth. Assist your child in navigating the ups and downs of life. Demonstrate faith in your kid's capacity for problem-solving and taking on new challenges.
- discipline in a positive, equitable, and consistent manner. Instead of inflicting physical harm, use discipline as a teaching method. Since every

child and family is unique, find out what works best for your child. Show support for admirable actions. Encourage your child to learn from mistakes.

- Love without conditions Instill the value of apologizing, working together, being patient, forgiving, and showing consideration for others.
- Be realistic about your expectations; being a parent is hard work.

CHAPTER 5

How does the environment affect the development of a child?

Young minds learn by observation, and parents are a child's first teachers. Thus, it could hurt your child's behavior and learning if you and your spouse frequently argue or live in a neighborhood where loud fights are a regular occurrence.

environmental elements that influence a child's development
Your child's overall development will not be constrained by what you teach them. Early learning is also influenced by the surroundings and environment in which your child is raised. It is particularly crucial during the formative years of life when the child is open to external stimuli and it greatly influences them. Environments at home, school, daycare, the neighborhood, and any other places where your child

spends a significant amount of time could all play a role.

The following environmental elements have an impact on your child's development:

1. Your emotional connection to your kid Environmental elements like parental emotional connection have an impact on a child's development.

The child's first environment is at home. Since the moment of their birth, their personalities have been shaped by the emotional surroundings they have experienced. Your relationship with your child will help them understand their feelings of love and fear and teach them how to do so.

They will learn how to communicate with people who are close to them from it. Early on, having a special relationship with you will give them a sense of security and assurance.

The personality of your child will be fostered by a secure and loving relationship. They'll experience significance and value.

Make sure you give them enough time to see your love for them. Always be there for them, and hold their hands.

Giving the child quality time is crucial for working mothers.

You might decide to schedule brief periods of one-on-one time for the child spread out evenly throughout the day.

2. Your partnership's equation

The development of children may be impacted by a couple's relationship.
Save

Your marriage will have an impact on your child's emotional and developmental growth.
The two people who will be closest to your child are possibly you and your spouse. Additionally, you two will be the first people your child ever meets.
Your child will learn about respecting other people from the way you interact with one another and from the love and affection you share as a couple.
They will understand the value of a solid connection and how to respect others.
A small amount of affectionate expression in front of your child is acceptable and required. Holding hands and giving a hug are simple but effective ways to demonstrate to your child that these are normal ways to show affection.

3. Your entire family
Family time with extended family can promote the growth of healthy children.

In the formative, vulnerable years of life, family time, particularly with a joint family, is essential to the development of the child and their developing brain.
Different aspects of their childhood experience will be influenced by the family's financial situation as well as their emotional connection. Your child may occasionally observe your spending and purchasing patterns and contrast them with those of people they are familiar with, such as their friends and friends' parents.
You must discuss these matters with your child while taking personal time, keeping in mind their perceptions and explaining them.

4. Television and social media
Promoting healthy screen time will aid in development.
Save

Nowadays, with everything available on a digital platform, exponentially rising screen times are not uncommon.
Parents serve as early-life role models for children, who absorb information like absorbent sponges.
Ensure you are not leading them to believe that the online world is superior to smartphones or laptops.
If you are unable to completely avoid screen time, you can use this weapon constructively during the advised times to streamline age-appropriate, kid-friendly, and educational information.

5. A setting for learning
To encourage your child's skill development, create a stimulating learning environment.
Image saved by iStock

It is crucial to create an environment that stimulates and supports your child's skill development because you are their first teacher.

6. Your child will learn more effectively and concentrate on their studies if they live in a happy and relaxed environment.

7. You and your partner should give your child the chance to explore, even in the house.
Encourage your child to seek answers and ask questions at all times. They will learn more as a result.

The main environmental elements influencing a child's development are the emotional ties between children and parents. Like a sponge, children soak up everything around them, and this starts to show in their personality and behavior. The family environment, social media, and television all affect how cognitively a child develops. Children who participate in family discussions may become more aware of family dynamics. Children need to be given time and attention as well, especially in joint families. Children gain the ability to express their fears and gain the respect, love, and care of their family members in this manner.